Easy Concert Pieces
Leichte Konzertstücke

for Descant (Soprano) Recorder and Piano
für Sopranblockflöte und Klavier

Volume 3 / Band 3

21 Pieces from 5 Centuries
21 Stücke aus 5 Jahrhunderten

Grade / Schwierigkeitsgrad:
intermediate / mittelschwer

Edited by / Herausgegeben von
Elisabeth Kretschmann

ED 23162
ISMN 979-0-001-20800-0

Volume 1 / Band 1:
very easy to easy / sehr leicht bis leicht
ED 23043

Volume 2 / Band 2:
easy to intermediate / leicht bis mittelschwer
ED 23044

www.schott-music.com

Mainz · London · Madrid · Paris · New York · Tokyo · Beijing

Preface

This series of *Easy Concert Pieces* presents easy to intermediate pieces for descant recorder, including original compositions alongside arrangements in a selection ranging across different eras. These pieces will provide an ideal complement to any recorder tutorial method: as well as providing material for tuition purposes they are particularly suitable for playing at auditions, competitions and examinations. Pieces are grouped in increasing order of difficulty in three volumes. Within each book pieces are presented in chronological order, starting with works from the Renaissance and early Baroque period and progressing through Baroque, Classical and Romantic periods to more modern music.

Book 1 contains short and easily manageable pieces with a range from c' to e" including semitones f♯' and b♭'. Rhythms are kept simple. Some of the pieces have a very limited range, so this book can be used as a source of material very soon after starting recorder lessons.

Book 2 extends the range of notes to a" and includes a few semitones. Pieces are rhythmically more complex and slightly more demanding with regard to fingering technique and melodic expression than the pieces in book 1.

Book 3 finally includes pieces using the whole range of notes. Longer pieces allow for more detailed musical phrasing with scope for individual interpretation and expression.

The accompanying CD includes all the pieces in the full version and as play-along piano accompaniment, too.

Elisabeth Kretschmann
Translation Julia Rushworth

Vorwort

Die Reihe *Easy Concert Pieces* enthält leichte bis mittelschwere Originalkompositionen sowie Bearbeitungen für Sopranblockflöte und Klavier und bietet einen Querschnitt durch verschiedene Epochen. Die ausgewählten Werke sind eine ideale Ergänzung zu jeder Blockflötenschule. Neben dem Unterricht eignen sie sich besonders gut für Vorspiele, Wettbewerbe und Prüfungen. Die Stücke wurden für die 3 Bände nach aufsteigendem Schwierigkeitsgrad angeordnet. Innerhalb eines Bandes finden sich die Werke in chronologischer Reihenfolge, angefangen bei Werken aus Renaissance und Frühbarock über Barock, Klassik und Romantik bis hin zu modernen Stücken.

In Band 1 befinden sich überschaubare kurze Stücke im Tonraum von c' bis e" einschließlich der Halbtöne fis' und b'. Die Rhythmik ist einfach gehalten. Einige Stücke haben nur einen geringen Ambitus, so dass dieser Band schon nach kurzer Zeit des Blockflötenunterrichts als Begleitheft Verwendung finden kann.

In Band 2 wird der Tonraum bis a" erweitert, einschließlich einiger Halbtöne. Die Werke sind rhythmisch komplexer gestaltet und stellen in Grifftechnik und melodischem Ausdruck etwas höhere Anforderungen als die Stücke aus Band 1.

In Band 3 wurden schließlich Werke aufgenommen, die den gesamten Tonraum nutzen. Die teils längeren Stücke ermöglichen eine musikalisch differenzierte Arbeit und fördern die eigene Interpretation und Ausdrucksstärke.

Die beigefügte CD enthält alle Stücke als Vollversion und als Klavierbegleitung zum Mitspielen.

Elisabeth Kretschmann

Impressum
Cover photography: © Mollenhauer-Blockflöten
CD: Elisabeth Kretschmann, Descant (Soprano) Recorder, Volker Krebs (Piano)
Recording: Studio Tonmeister, Mainz (Nos. 1–8, 10–11, 14, 16–21)
Gunni Mahling, Saarbrücken (Nos. 9, 12–13, 15)

Printed in Germany · BSS 59575

Contents / Inhalt

pitch a / Stimmton a (Track No. 43)

1. Sonata terza

Tomaso Cecchino
1583–1644
Arr.: Hugo Ruf

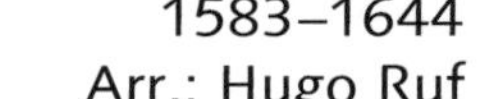

♩ ca. 120

from / aus: T. Cecchino, 3 Sonatas, Schott OFB 159

17
21
25
29

34
40
45
49
54
1.
2.
6
#

2. Corrente

Girolamo Frescobaldi
1583–1643
Arr. Gwilym Beechey

from / aus: G. Frescobaldi, 4 Correntes (No. 3), Schott ED 12276

16
22
28
33
1.
2.
1.
2.

3. Adagio

Johann Christoph Pepusch
1667–1752
Arr.: Gustav Lenzewski

from / aus: J. Chr. Pepusch, Sonata No. 2 D minor / d-Moll
CD: without repeats / ohne Wiederholungen

4. Allegro

Diogenio Bigaglia
ca. 1676–ca. 1745
Basso continuo: Hugo Ruf

from / aus: D. Bigaglia, Sonata A minor / a-Moll, Schott OFB 3
CD: without repeats / ohne Wiederholungen

37
43
51
57
tr

CD: without repeats / ohne Wiederholungen

5. Allegro

Jean Baptiste Loeillet
1680–1730
Arr.: Vera Mohrs

♩ ca. 80

4

8

12

from / aus: J. B. Loeillet, Sonata C major / C-Dur
CD: without repeats / ohne Wiederholungen

16
tr
19
23
27
tr

30
tr
tr
33
36
39

6. Tambourin

Louis de Caix d'Hervelois
ca. 1680–1759
Arr.: Vera Mohrs

from / aus: L. de Caix d'Hervelois, Suite op. 6/4

7. Siciliana

Georg Philipp Telemann
1681–1767
Arr.: Walter Bergmann

from / aus: G. Ph. Telemann, Partita No. 2 in G, Schott OFB 1003

12
16
20
24

8. Aria

Georg Philipp Telemann
Arr.: Walter Bergmann

from / aus: G. Ph. Telemann, Partita No. 2 in G, Schott OFB 1003 (Aria 1)
CD: without repeats / ohne Wiederholungen

1. Sonata terza

Tomaso Cecchino
1583–1644

♩ ca. 120

8

13 ♩ = 𝅗𝅥

18 𝅗𝅥 = ♩

23

29

34 ♩ = 𝅗𝅥

38 𝅗𝅥 = ♩

42

48

54

1. 2.

from / aus: T. Cecchino, 3 Sonatas, Schott OFB 159

2. Corrente

Girolamo Frescobaldi
1583–1643

from / aus: G. Frescobaldi, 4 Correntes (No. 3), Schott ED 12276

3. Adagio

Johann Christoph Pepusch
1667–1752

from / aus: J. Chr. Pepusch, Sonata No. 2 D minor / d-Moll
CD: without repeats / ohne Wiederholungen

4 25

4. Allegro

Diogenio Bigaglia
ca. 1676 – ca. 1745

from / aus: D. Bigaglia, Sonata A minor / a-Moll, Schott OFB 3
CD: without repeats / ohne Wiederholungen

5. Allegro

Jean Baptiste Loeillet
1680–1730

♩ ca. 80

from / aus: J. B. Loeillet, Sonata C major / C-Dur
CD: without repeats / ohne Wiederholungen

6 | 27

6. Tambourin

Louis de Caix d'Hervelois
ca. 1680–1759

from / aus: L. de Caix d'Hervelois, Suite op. 6/4

7 | 28

7. Siciliana

Georg Philipp Telemann
1681–1767

♩ ca. 142

5

9

13

18

23

from / aus: G. Ph. Telemann, Partita No. 2 in G, Schott OFB 1003

8. Aria

Georg Philipp Telemann

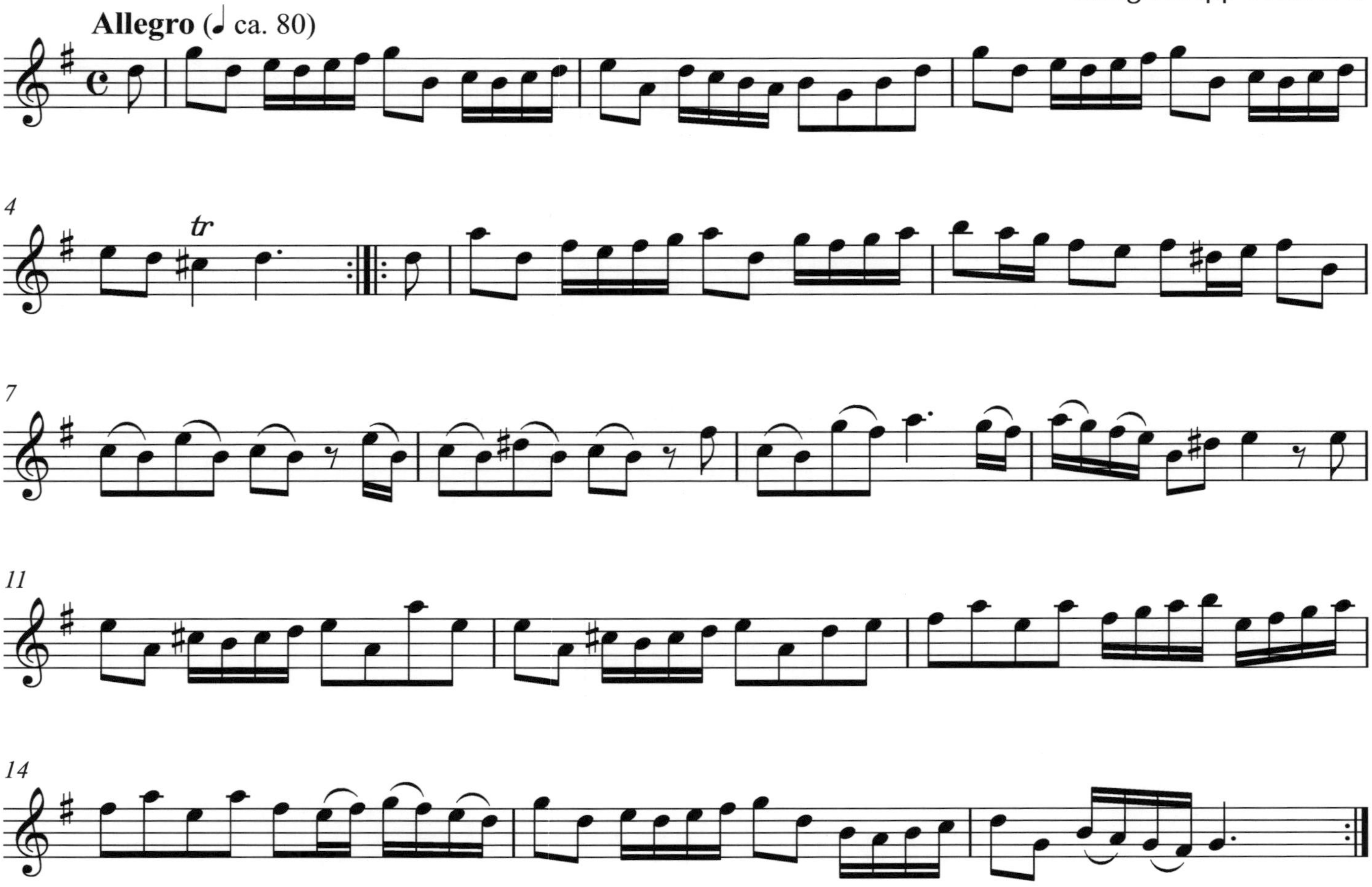

Allegro (♩ ca. 80)

tr

from / aus: G. Ph. Telemann, Partita No. 2 in G, Schott OFB 1003 (Aria 1)
CD: without repeats / ohne Wiederholungen

9. Andante

Joseph Haydn
1732–1809

from / aus: J. Haydn, Surprise Symphony, No. 94 / Sinfonie mit dem Paukenschlag, Nr. 94

10 31

10. Andante

James Hook
1746–1827

from / aus: J. Hook, Sonata G major / G-Dur, Schott ED 10108
CD: without repeats / ohne Wiederholungen

11. Minuet / Menuett

Luigi Boccherini
1743–1805

12. The Bird Catcher's Song

„Der Vogelfänger bin ich ja"

Wolfgang Amadeus Mozart
1756–1791

from / aus: W. A: Mozart, The Magic Flute / Die Zauberflöte
*) Piano ad lib. instead of recorder / Klavier ad lib. statt Blockflöte

13 34

13. Für Elise
(Theme / Thema)

Ludwig van Beethoven
1770–1827

14 35

14. Habanera

Georges Bizet
1838–1875

15. To a Wild Rose

Edward MacDowell
1860–1908

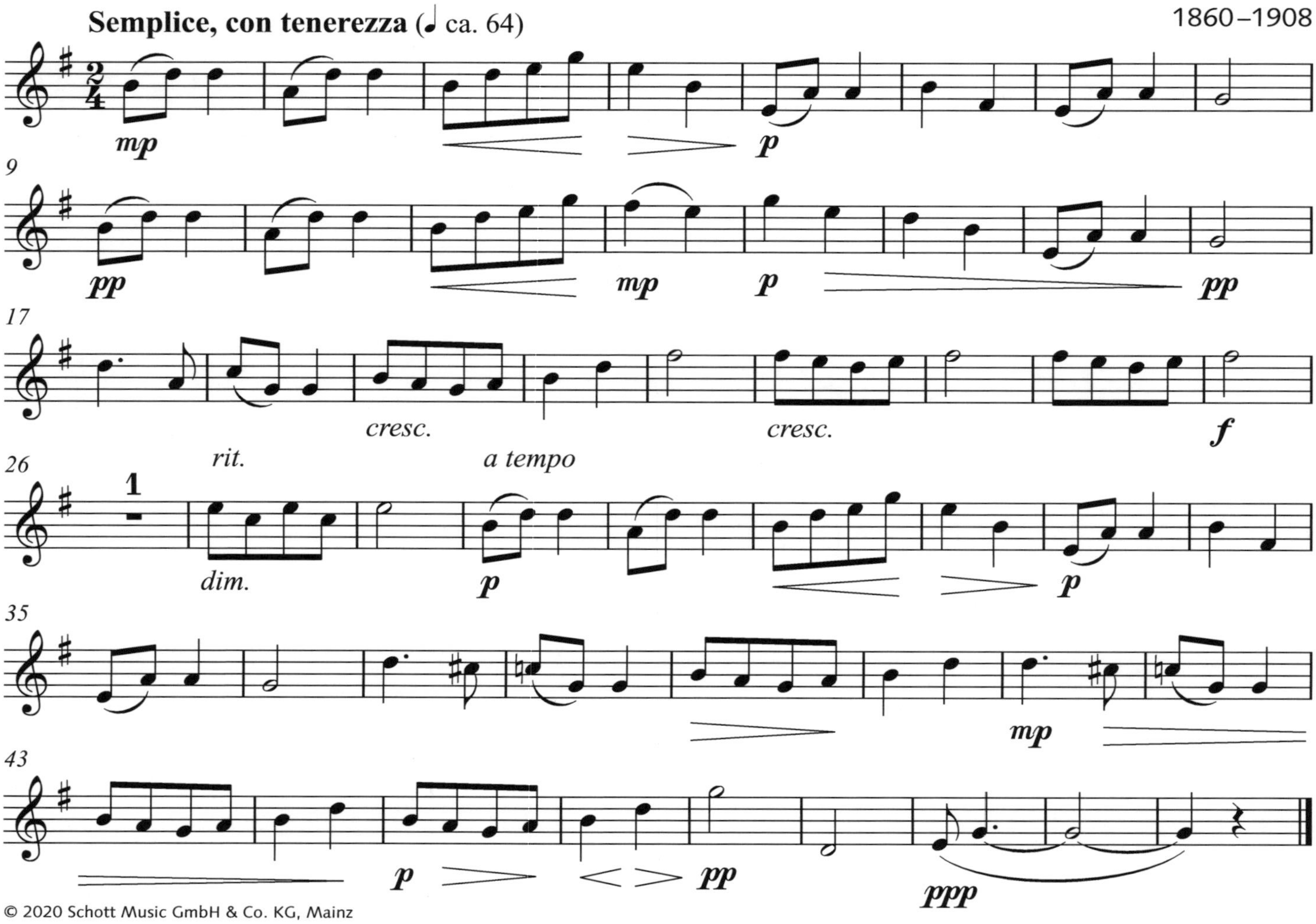

Semplice, con tenerezza (♩ ca. 64)

mp *p*

9

pp *mp* *p* *pp*

17

cresc. *cresc.* *f*

26

rit. *a tempo*

1

dim. *p* *p*

35

mp

43

p *pp* *ppp*

from /aus: E. MacDowell, Woodland Sketches / Amerikanische Wald-Idyllen, op. 51/1

16. Ragtime

17. The Mouse / Die Maus

Theme from / Titelmusik aus „Die Sendung mit der Maus"

Hans Posegga
1917–2002

18. Meadow in the Morning Sun

Wiese in der Morgensonne

Werner Rottler
1939–2012

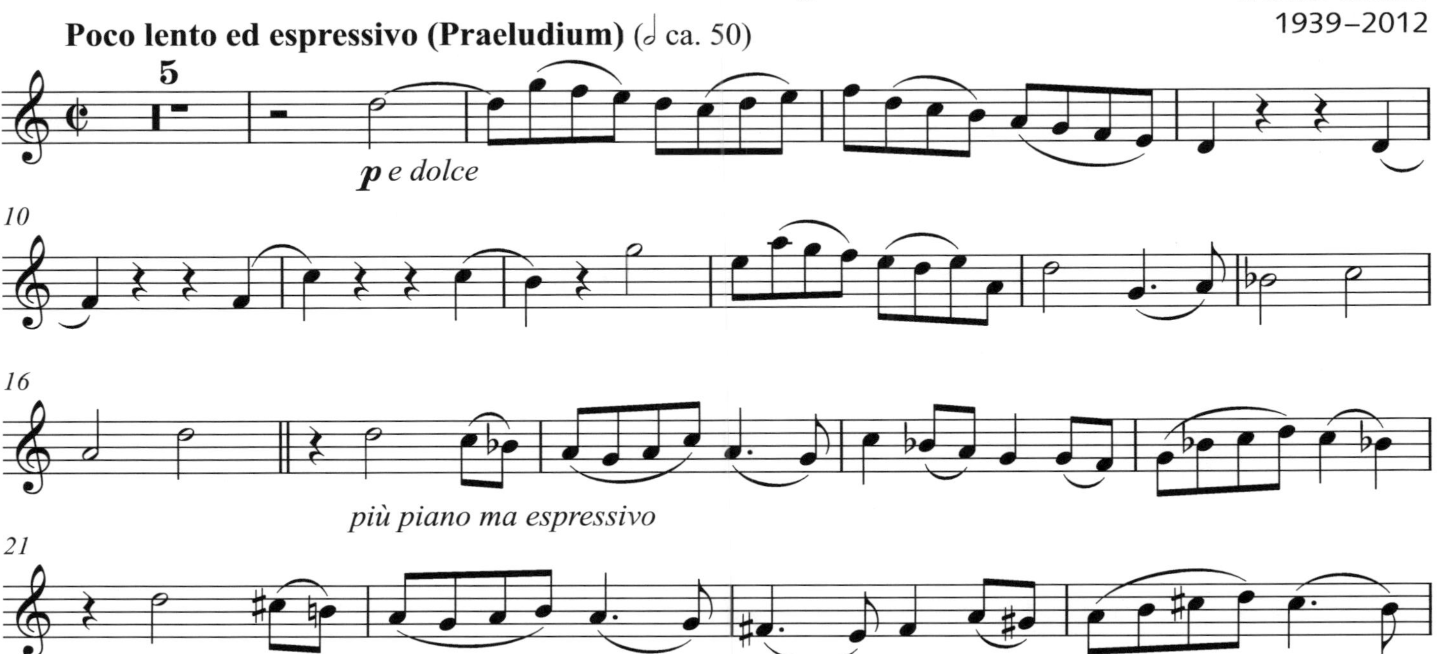

from / aus: W. Rottler, A beasty pleasure / Ein tierisches Vergnügen, Möseler MOS 22605

25 *poco rit.*

31 **Tempo I** *poco rit.*

p *p e dolce*

37

42 *rit.*

19 40

19. Feeling Blue

Rainer Mohrs
*1953

Moderato (♩ ca. 104) ♫ = ♩♪ (triplet)

8 1

15 (2. x Improvisation *ad lib.*)

1

20

Fine

25

31

36

D. C. al Fine

20. Feeling Happy

Rainer Mohrs

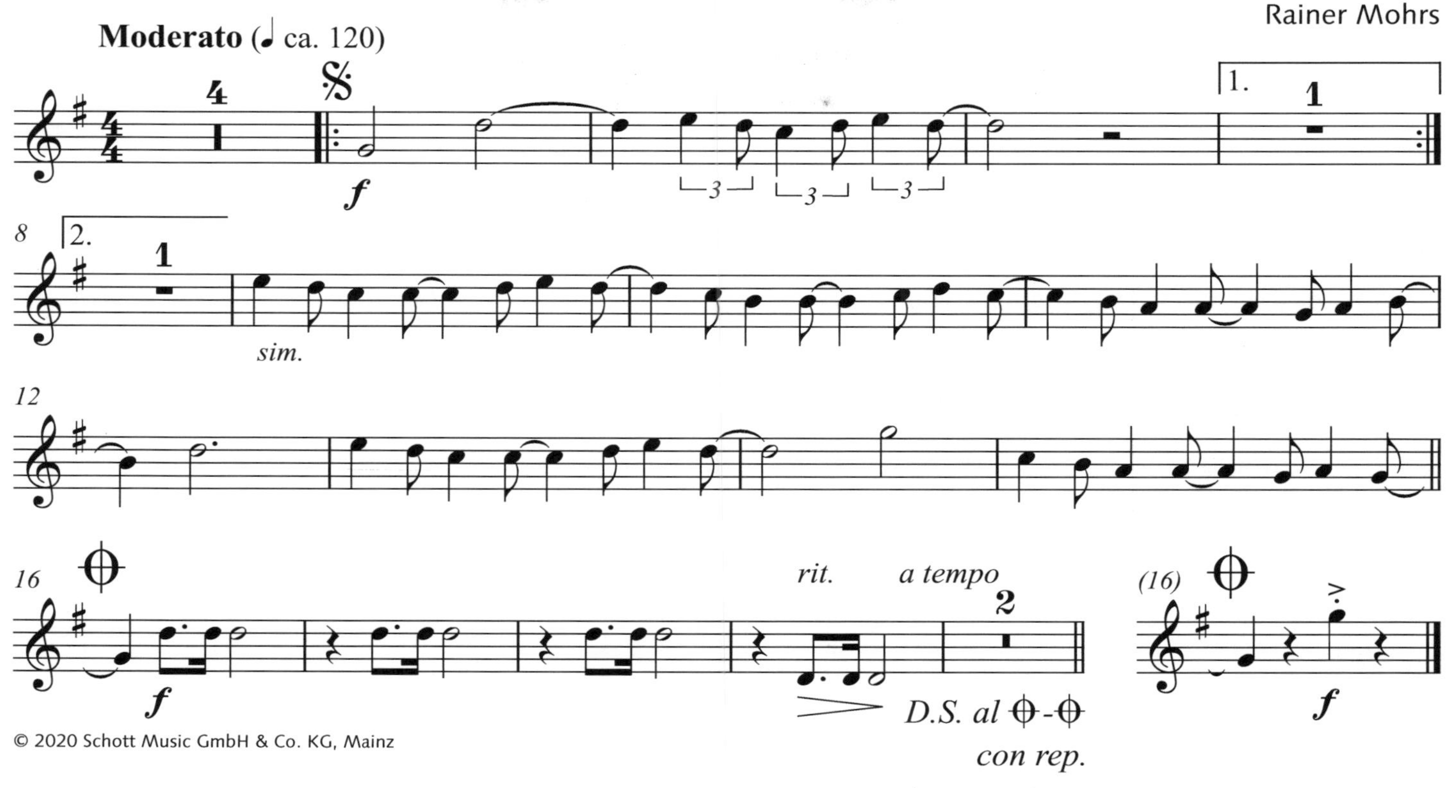

21. The Bat's Swing / Fledermaus-Swing

Hans-Georg Lotz
1934–2001

from / aus: H.-G. Lotz, Dachboden-Suite, Möseler MOS 41184

Contents / Inhalt

Preface

This series of *Easy Concert Pieces* presents easy to intermediate pieces for descant recorder, including original compositions alongside arrangements in a selection ranging across different eras. These pieces will provide an ideal complement to any recorder tutorial method: as well as providing material for tuition purposes they are particularly suitable for playing at auditions, competitions and examinations. Pieces are grouped in increasing order of difficulty in three volumes. Within each book pieces are presented in chronological order, starting with works from the Renaissance and early Baroque period and progressing through Baroque, Classical and Romantic periods to more modern music.

Book 1 contains short and easily manageable pieces with a range from c' to e" including semitones f♯' and b♭'. Rhythms are kept simple. Some of the pieces have a very limited range, so this book can be used as a source of material very soon after starting recorder lessons.

Book 2 extends the range of notes to a" and includes a few semitones. Pieces are rhythmically more complex and slightly more demanding with regard to fingering technique and melodic expression than the pieces in book 1.

Book 3 finally includes pieces using the whole range of notes. Longer pieces allow for more detailed musical phrasing with scope for individual interpretation and expression.

The accompanying CD includes all the pieces in the full version and as play-along piano accompaniment, too.

Elisabeth Kretschmann
Translation Julia Rushworth

Vorwort

Die Reihe *Easy Concert Pieces* enthält leichte bis mittelschwere Originalkompositionen sowie Bearbeitungen für Sopranblockflöte und Klavier und bietet einen Querschnitt durch verschiedene Epochen. Die ausgewählten Werke sind eine ideale Ergänzung zu jeder Blockflötenschule. Neben dem Unterricht eignen sie sich besonders gut für Vorspiele, Wettbewerbe und Prüfungen. Die Stücke wurden für die 3 Bände nach aufsteigendem Schwierigkeitsgrad angeordnet. Innerhalb eines Bandes finden sich die Werke in chronologischer Reihenfolge, angefangen bei Werken aus Renaissance und Frühbarock über Barock, Klassik und Romantik bis hin zu modernen Stücken.

In Band 1 befinden sich überschaubare kurze Stücke im Tonraum von c' bis e" einschließlich der Halbtöne fis' und b'. Die Rhythmik ist einfach gehalten. Einige Stücke haben nur einen geringen Ambitus, so dass dieser Band schon nach kurzer Zeit des Blockflötenunterrichts als Begleitheft Verwendung finden kann.

In Band 2 wird der Tonraum bis a" erweitert, einschließlich einiger Halbtöne. Die Werke sind rhythmisch komplexer gestaltet und stellen in Grifftechnik und melodischem Ausdruck etwas höhere Anforderungen als die Stücke aus Band 1.

In Band 3 wurden schließlich Werke aufgenommen, die den gesamten Tonraum nutzen. Die teils längeren Stücke ermöglichen eine musikalisch differenzierte Arbeit und fördern die eigene Interpretation und Ausdrucksstärke.

Die beigefügte CD enthält alle Stücke als Vollversion und als Klavierbegleitung zum Mitspielen.

Elisabeth Kretschmann

Easy Concert Pieces
Leichte Konzertstücke

for Descant (Soprano) Recorder and Piano
für Sopranblockflöte und Klavier

Volume 3 / Band 3

21 Pieces from 5 Centuries
21 Stücke aus 5 Jahrhunderten

Grade / Schwierigkeitsgrad:
intermediate / mittelschwer

Edited by / Herausgegeben von
Elisabeth Kretschmann

ED 23162
ISMN 979-0-001-20800-0

Volume 1 / Band 1:
very easy to easy / sehr leicht bis leicht
ED 23043

Volume 2 / Band 2:
easy to intermediate / leicht bis mittelschwer
ED 23044

Descant (Soprano) Recorder

www.schott-music.com

Mainz · London · Madrid · Paris · New York · Tokyo · Beijing

9. Andante

Joseph Haydn
1732–1809
Arr.: Wolfgang Birtel

from / aus: J. Haydn, Surprise Symphony, No. 94 / Sinfonie mit dem Paukenschlag, Nr. 94

10. Andante

James Hook
1746–1827
Arr.: Walter Bergmann

from / aus: J. Hook, Sonata G major / G-Dur, Schott ED 10108
CD: without repeats / ohne Wiederholungen

27
32
rit.
a tempo
rit.
a tempo
38
44
49

11. Minuet / Menuett

Luigi Boccherini
1743–1805
Arr.: Elisabeth Kretschmann

12. The Bird Catcher's Song

„Der Vogelfänger bin ich ja“

Wolfgang Amadeus Mozart
1756–1791
Arr.: Wolfgang Birtel

from / aus: W. A: Mozart, The Magic Flute / Die Zauberflöte
*) Piano ad lib. instead of recorder / Klavier ad lib. statt Blockflöte

13. Für Elise

(Theme / Thema)

Ludwig van Beethoven
1770–1827
Arr.: Elisabeth Kretschmann

14. Habanera

Georges Bizet
1838–1875
Arr.: Elisabeth Kretschmann

15. To a Wild Rose

Edward MacDowell
1860–1908
Arr.: Wolfgang Birtel

from / aus: E. MacDowell, Woodland Sketches / Amerikanische Wald-Idyllen, op. 51/1

rit.
a tempo
dim.
p
dim.
p
p
p
mp
mp
poco marcato
p
pp
ppp
p
pp
ppp

16. Ragtime

Mátyás Seiber
1905–1960
Arr.: Elisabeth Kretschmann

17. The Mouse / Die Maus

Theme from / Titelmusik aus „Die Sendung mit der Maus"

Hans Posegga
1917–2002
Arr.: Elisabeth Kretschmann

18. Meadow in the Morning Sun

Wiese in der Morgensonne

Werner Rottler
1939–2012

from / aus: W. Rottler, A beasty pleasure / Ein tierisches Vergnügen, Möseler MOS 22605
*) Notation simplified: play as rhythmic arpeggio / Notation vereinfacht: denke rhythmisiertes Arpeggio

22
27
poco rit.
poco rit.
Tempo I
p
p
32
p e dolce
37
42
rit.
rit.

19. Feeling Blue

Rainer Mohrs
*1953

21
mp
f
Fine
25
mf
sim.
31
36
D. C. al Fine

20. Feeling Happy

Rainer Mohrs

13
16
f
f
rit.
a tempo
poco rit.
a tempo
3
20
mf
sim.
(16)
f
f
D.S. al ⊕-⊕ con rep.

21. The Bat's Swing / Fledermaus-Swing

Hans-Georg Lotz
1934–2001

from / aus: H.-G. Lotz, Dachboden-Suite, Möseler MOS 41184